special forces

Adam
Sutherland

Lerner Publications Company
Minneapolis

First American edition published in 2012
by Lerner Publishing Group, Inc. Published
by arrangement with Wayland, a division of
Hachette Children's Books

Lerner Publications Company
A division of Lerner Publishing Group, Inc.
241 First Avenue North
Minneapolis, MN U.S.A.

Website address: www.lernerbooks.com

Library of Congress Cataloging-in-Publication Data

Sutherland, Adam.
    Special forces / by Adam Sutherland.
        p.   cm. — (On the radar: defend and
        protect)
    Includes index.
    ISBN 978-0-7613-7772-6 (lib. bdg. : alk. paper)
    1. Special forces (Military science)—Juvenile
literature. I. Title.
U262.S88 2012
356'.609731—dc23   2011023218

Manufactured in the United States of America
1 - CG - 12/31/11

Acknowledgments: Alamy: Homer Sykes Archive 17; Corbis:
Leif Skoogfors 4–5; Dreamstime: Vampy1 9; Flickr: Uniquely
Elite 6b; iStock: Allkindza 2tc, 8; Shutterstock: 1971yes 18–19,
Garret Bautista 3br, Ryan Rodrick Beiler 13l, Ramon Berk
21bl, Sascha Hahn back cover, Homeros 3l, 16–17, Hurricane
2tr, 22–23, Sarah Kinnel 30–31, Kletr 21br, Leenvdb 26–27,
Katarzyna Mazurowska cover, TebNad 14–15; U.S. Army: 2b,
21bc; U.S. Navy: 1, 2–3, 7r, 11, 24–25, 25; Wikimedia: Folutil
12l, Saperaud 12r, U.S. Army 12r, 13r, 26, US National Guard
28–29, US Air Force 17b.

Main body text set in
Helvetica Neue LT Std 13/15.5.
Typeface provided by Adobe Systems.

cover stories

thepeople

themachines

themoves

thetalk

COMBAT TALK

Learn some special forces lingo with our On the Radar guide.

airstrike
an attack from the air on a specific target by military aircraft

amphibious
military operations launched from the water against an enemy shore

antiterrorist/ counter- terrorism
the methods used by governments to prevent terrorist attacks

caliber
the diameter of a shell or bullet

camouflage
a pattern used to blend into the surroundings

carbine
a lightweight rifle

deploy
to position something, usually troops or parachutes, ready for action

foxhole
a small pit dug to provide shelter, usually against enemy fire

intelligence gathering
collecting information on enemies' strengths and weaknesses, and assessing their likely future actions

Kevlar
a light, strong material used in protective army clothing

marksmanship
shooting skills

mine
an explosive device

mortar
a type of weapon that fires shells over short distances

platoon
between two and four squads of soldiers, usually led by a lieutenant (a squad contains eight to 13 soldiers)

radar
a system that uses radio waves to spot aircraft or other objects that are not visible to the eye

rebel forces
an unofficial army, usually fighting for the removal of its country's government

A tough entry program makes sure that only the best fighters make it into the special forces.

reconnaissance
getting information about an enemy's position

tear gas
a nonlethal gas that temporarily irritates the eyes, the nose, the mouth, and the lungs

stun grenades
nonlethal explosives that give off a bright flash of light and a very loud blast to temporarily affect an enemy's sight, hearing, and balance

warlord
a leader of a rebel force, who holds power through military force

Special forces recruits learn to rappel as part of their training.

GLOSSARY

elite
the most powerful or skilled members of a group

influential
important, powerful, respected

interrogation
being questioned with the goal of obtaining important, often secret, information

joint venture
a business partnership

national security
the safety of a country

NATO
short for the North Atlantic Treaty Organization, a group of countries that works together to protect one another

al-Qaeda
an extreme Islamic group founded by Osama bin Laden

rappel
to go down a rock face or building using ropes

rehabilitating
recovering from injury or illness

simulator
something that re-creates an experience, such as a terrorist situation

terrain
a type of ground surface

vertebrae
the bones in the neck and the back

The dramatic announcement of bin Laden's death made headlines.

THE HUNT FOR BIN LADEN

The world's most wanted man was captured and killed in 2011 by SEAL Team Six in northern Pakistan. But how did they find him and carry out their mission?

This model shows how SEAL helicopters landed in the Abbottabad compound without being seen.

LOCATING BIN LADEN

U.S. forces had been searching for Osama bin Laden since 9/11 (September 11, 2001), the day his al-Qaeda supporters crashed airplanes in New York, near Washington, D.C., and in Pennsylvania, killing thousands of people. Several captured members of al-Qaeda mentioned the name Abu Ahmed al-Kuwaiti as one of bin Laden's most trusted allies. The United States would be closer to finding bin Laden if al-Kuwaiti was found. Al-Kuwaiti was eventually tracked to a compound in Abbottabad, Pakistan. But even then, U.S. officials were not entirely sure that bin Laden was hiding in Abbottabad.

THE PLAN

President Barack Obama had one of his toughest decisions to make. He could wait for more information to confirm bin Laden's presence, bomb the building from the air, or launch a small-scale attack. In the end, he chose a helicopter attack to reduce the number of civilian casualties and to hopefully provide evidence that bin Laden was inside. SEAL Team Six was chosen for the raid and spent several weeks training for the attack in a full-size model of the Abbottabad compound.

INTO BATTLE

On the night of May 1, 2011, two SEAL teams totaling 24 men arrived at the compound in two Black Hawk helicopters. One of the helicopters lost height and crashed, but the SEALs escaped uninjured. They entered the compound and then killed al-Kuwaiti; bin Laden's son, Khalid; and bin Laden. They took bin Laden's body, plus 10 computer hard drives and other evidence, and were back in the air within 38 minutes—an outstanding special forces operation.

WORLD'S BEST FIGHTERS

Special forces date back thousands of years. They were special because they had more training, experience, better equipment, and more... than regular troops.

Roman emperors such as Justinian I *(center)* relied on their bodyguards *(pictured to his left)* to protect them from assassination.

ANCIENT BODYGUARDS

In around 550 B.C., a Persian elite group called the Immortals served as the king's bodyguard. The world's oldest fighting unit, it had 10,000 men. Anyone who died in battle was replaced immediately. In ancient Rome, from 280 B.C. to A.D. 476, the Praetorian Guard had the same role: protecting the emperor and defending the city.

AMERICANS IN ACTION

In the 1600s and the 1700s, warfare in what became the eastern United States involved small units of Native Americans or colonial soldiers. They were able to fight in short bursts on difficult terrain. During the Revolutionary War (1775–1783), the Continental Army fought the British Army in large-scale battles. But hit-and-run tactics also were effective. Since then, special operations have been part of every war involving the United States. U.S. Rangers and navy scouts brought their special ops skills to World War II (1939–1945). Green Berets fought in the Korean War (1950–1953). SEALs got their start as a special unit in the 1960s. By the 1970s, Delta Force had become a counterterrorist threat.

BRITISH ARMY IN AFRICA

Colonel David Stirling formed the SAS in 1941. It was made up of soldiers trained to operate in small teams behind enemy lines. Its first operation, a parachute jump into North Africa, was a disaster. One-third of the 65 men taking part were captured or killed. However, the missions that followed were far more successful. The SAS inspired other nations to develop similar special forces.

Special forces training has developed over recent years to ensure that troops can carry out operations in harsh terrain all over the world.

WARFARE ON THE WATER

In 1962 President John Kennedy sent the first two U.S. Navy SEAL teams to fight in Vietnam. They were known as the men with green faces by the opposing army because of their camouflage face paint. The teams specialized in gathering intelligence and getting in and out of enemy territory without being spotted.

The war on terror

Delta Force was formed in 1977 by Charles Beckwith, a U.S. Army special forces officer who had spent a year training with the SAS. When he returned to the United States, Beckwith persuaded the U.S. government to form a similar unit to protect against the growing threat of terrorism. Delta Force has been involved in many important operations since the 1990s.

PASSPORT TO PROTECTION

Successful Spetsnaz candidates receive a badge with an eagle emblem *(left)* upon completion of their training. German special forces are trained to operate in secret behind enemy lines *(above)*.

Most countries have at least one specially trained elite force, designed to fight in foreign conflicts and to protect against enemy attack at home. Here are some of the most influential forces from around the world.

THE RUSSIAN SUPER FORCE

Fewer than 2 in 10 candidates pass the Russian special forces (Spetsnaz) selection process. Around 15,000 troops work across different government departments, but their job is the same—counterterrorism and national security. The Spetsnaz GRU are the elite of the elite. This small, highly trained Russian army unit was formed after World War II and has fought in Iraq and Afghanistan.

GERMANY'S ELITE CORPS

The German Special Forces Command (Kommando Spezialkräfte) was formed in 1997 and is modeled after the U.S. Delta Force and the British SAS. The unit of around 450 men has been honored by

The IDF *(below left)* patrols the West Bank border to protect Israel from Palestinian attacks. The Japanese Special Forces Group *(below right)* is currently serving in Iraq.

NATO for its outstanding service in Bosnia and Kosovo during the conflicts that took place there in the 1990s. The Special Forces Command currently has troops serving in Afghanistan.

BATTLE IN THE MIDDLE EAST

The Israel Defense Forces (IDF) are an undercover force that focuses on antiterrorist operations on the West Bank (the border area between Israel and Palestine). It is known to be one of the world's most successful counterterrorism units.

ASIAN FORCES

The Japanese Special Forces Group is Japan's version of the Delta Force. This

small group of just 300 soldiers is drawn from the country's Narashino Airborne Brigade and is responsible for protecting Japan from terrorist attacks.

THE FORCE DOWN UNDER

The Special Air Service Regiment (SASR) in Australia is modeled after the British SAS. The three squadrons have fought in major world conflicts, including Vietnam, Iraq, and Afghanistan. The regiment has two specific roles—reconnaissance and hostage rescue.

13

SUPER CHOPPERS

Helicopters are the special forces' transport of choice. They are super-fast and can land on difficult terrain almost anywhere in the world!

UH-60L BLACK HAWK

Twin-engine helicopter used by U.S. special forces

Cruising speed: 173 mph/278 kph
Combat range: 368 mi./592 km
Rotor diameter: 53 ft. 8 in./16.36 m
Length: 64 ft. 10 in./19.76 m
Maximum takeoff weight: 23,500 lb./10,660 kg
Crew: 4

CH-53D SEA STALLION

Twin-engine transport helicopter used by the U.S. Navy, the U.S. Marines, and the U.S. Air Force

Cruising speed: 173 mph/278 kph
Combat range: 100 mi./160 km
Rotor diameter: 72 ft. 3 in./22 m
Length: 88.5 ft./27 m
Maximum takeoff weight: 42,000 lb./19,051 kg
Crew: 3

AH-64A APACHE

Twin-engine attack helicopter used by U.S. and British special forces

Cruising speed: 165 mph/265 kph
Combat range: 300 mi./483 km
Rotor diameter: 48 ft./14.63 m
Length: 58.17 ft./17.73 m
Maximum takeoff weight: 23,000 lb./10,433 kg
Crew: 2

AH-1W SUPER COBRA

Twin-engine attack helicopter used
by the U.S. Marine Corps

Maximum speed:	218 mph/352 kph
Combat range:	365 mi./587 km
Rotor diameter:	48 ft./14.6 m
Length:	58 ft./17.7 m
Maximum takeoff weight:	14,750 lb./6,690 kg
Crew:	2

OH-58D KIOWA WARRIOR

Single-engine armed
reconnaissance helicopter
used by U.S. special forces

Cruising speed:	127 mph/204 kph
Combat range:	345 mi./555 km
Rotor diameter:	35 ft./10.7 m
Length:	42 ft. 2 in./12.9 m
Maximum takeoff weight:	5,500 lb./2,495 kg
Crew:	2

THE MISSIONS

Special forces operations are quick and decisive. Troops are known for taking on impossible odds and succeeding. Check out some of the most famous missions.

1. OPERATION NIFTY PACKAGE

In December 1989, President George H. W. Bush sent troops to invade Panama in Central America. Three Navy SEAL platoons (48 men) were given the job of capturing the country's oppressive dictator, Manuel Noriega. Noriega's private airplane and gunboat were both destroyed to prevent him from leaving the country. He was eventually captured and imprisoned for money laundering of drug money.

2. OPERATION RED DAWN

On December 13, 2003, Task Force 121—including members of Delta Force and the U.S. Army Rangers—captured Iraqi president Saddam Hussein. Hussein was discovered in a one-man foxhole, armed with an AK-47 rifle and holding $750,000 in cash. The Iraqi government tried and convicted him for crimes against humanity. He was given the death penalty and was executed in 2006.

3. OPERATION NIMROD

In April 1980, six armed terrorists entered the Iranian Embassy in London, England, taking 26 hostages. After five days, terrorists killed one hostage, and the British government decided to send in the SAS. Eight SAS men wearing gas masks and black uniforms rappelled from the embassy roof, threw in stun grenades and tear gas canisters, and entered the building. All but one terrorist was killed, and the hostages were freed.

4. OPERATION BARRAS

In September 2000, 11 British soldiers were taken prisoner by rebel forces in Sierra Leone, West Africa. Five of the soldiers were soon released, but negotiations broke down and rebels threatened to kill the remaining hostages. SAS and Special Boat Service troops were flown in to attack the rebel camps and free the British soldiers. They were in and out of the rebel camp with their mission completed in about 20 minutes!

5. THE BATTLE OF MOGADISHU

In October 1993, Delta Force and U.S. Ranger teams attempted to capture the Somali warlord Mohamed Farrah Aidid. Two Black Hawk helicopters were shot down by enemy fire in the center of rebel-held Mogadishu, Somalia. The troops' amazing escape was recorded in the book *Black Hawk Down* and later made into a Hollywood film.

THE HALO

High-altitude/low-opening (HALO) parachute jumps are an essential special forces skill. If weather conditions are calm, HALO jumps are a fast and reliable way to get troops and equipment into enemy territory.

Essential technique

- Jump cleanly from the aircraft
- Act quickly to locate jumping partners in midair
- Navigate accurately to locate the drop zone
- Land skillfully to avoid impact injuries

HOW IT'S DONE

1. The aircraft carrying the troops flies low into the target area to avoid being spotted on radar. It then goes up quickly to allow troops to jump.
2. The teams jump at night, using oxygen masks to help them breathe.
3. Small groups, usually four men, link together in the air by holding one another's arms. They fly in this formation for long distances, navigating by using a compass.
4. When they are at about 2,000 feet (609 m) from the ground, the troops open their parachutes for landing.

WHY DO IT?

HALO parachute jumps allow special forces troops to land unnoticed in enemy territory. Most radar systems cannot find parachutists. Troops can travel such long distances through the air that even if a HALO drop is discovered, it is impossible to accurately plot where the forces will eventually land.

DAVE THOMAS

Dave served in the 21st Regiment of the SAS for eight years. Read on for the inside scoop on what being in the SAS is like and what makes its selection procedure so tough!

What makes an SAS member so special?

You've got to have the right mental attitude. Being physically fit is very important. But operating behind enemy lines in extreme weather conditions—often with little or no sleep and under constant threat of capture—takes mental toughness too.

How hard is the selection process?

Extremely hard! If you pass the first few days of gym work and interviews, you end up at a two-week selection camp. Over the first three days, you do a 13.5-mile [22 km] timed walk, a 16.5-mile [27 km] timed walk and then, on the third day, a 34-mile [55 km] timed walk, called the Long Drag. Make it through those, and you stand a chance of succeeding!

What did you do to prepare for it?

I had read as much as I could about the SAS, so I knew it was going to be tough. I trained as best as I could. I'd run with a 45-pound [20 kg] backpack and carry two bricks in my hands to prepare me for the weapon I'd be carrying during real training!

What else do you learn during training?

You learn tactics, how to use weapons, how to parachute jump, and how to withstand enemy questioning. You are given a false identity that you are supposed to use when you are being interrogated. The idea is to drag out the questioning for as long as possible to increase the chance of being rescued.

What do you think inspires people to join the SAS and other elite forces?

To be the very best. The year before I joined, 212 men took the course and only 2 passed! The training pushes you mentally and physically to the limits. It's one of the toughest tests in the world.

FIREARMS STATS!

SMITH & WESSON 340 PD

Ultralight, short-barrel revolver designed and made in the United States

Used by:	U.S. special forces
Length:	6.31 in/16 cm
Weight (unloaded):	12 oz/340 g
Caliber:	.357 Magnum/9.1 mm
Number of rounds:	5

Special forces travel and work in small groups, so their weapons are chosen to be light, powerful, and reliable. Compare these handguns!

M9

Semiautomatic pistol designed by Beretta in Italy and made by Beretta USA

Used by:	U.S. special forces
Length:	8.5 in/21.7 cm
Weight (unloaded):	33.6 oz/952.5 g
Caliber:	.355 in/9 mm
Number of rounds:	15

KEY
cm = centimeters
mm = millimeters
g = grams

SIG SAUER P226 NAVY

Semiautomatic pistol designed by a Swiss (SIG) and German (Sauer) joint venture

Used by: U.S. Navy SEALs

Length: 7.7 in/19.6 cm

Weight (unloaded): 34.4 oz/975 g

Caliber: .355 in/9 mm

Number of rounds: 15

FN FIVE-SEVEN

Semiautomatic pistol designed and manufactured by FN Herstal in Belgium

Used by: U.S. Secret Service, Canadian special forces, Belgian special forces, and others

Length: 8.2 in/20.8 cm

Weight (unloaded): 21.8 oz/617 g

Caliber: .224 in/5.7 mm

Number of rounds: 20

GLOCK 17

Lightweight plastic semiautomatic pistol designed by Glock Ges in Austria

Used by: FBI, U.S. Marshals, and many U.S. state and local police departments

Length: 7.32 in/18.6 cm

Weight (unloaded): 22.2 oz/630 g

Caliber: .355 in/9 mm

Number of rounds: 17

UNDERWATER GEAR

helmet

mask

Navy SEALs travel light to get in and out of enemy territory quickly and without being seen. Their equipment plays an important role in the success of any mission.

HEADGEAR

When a SEAL is underwater, he wears a face mask and a rubber helmet. Out of the water, he wears a bullet-resistant Kevlar helmet with night-vision goggles and a communications headset. The headset allows SEALs to communicate with one another and with the base camp.

flipper

STAYING DRY

Sensitive equipment—such as weapons, explosives, and communication systems—need to be protected in a waterproof backpack. The backpack includes a SEAL's breathing gear. The pack can be inflated or deflated to help divers rise to the surface or swim to depths of up to 260 feet (80 m), depending on their mission.

ARMED AND DANGEROUS

SEALs will usually carry a handgun—often a SIG Sauer P226—as well as a SEAL team knife, with part-serrated and part-plain blade. The knife can be used in hand-to-hand combat or to cut through ropes or plants that might snare a diver underwater. SEALs also often carry an M4 carbine rifle, which is also effective at close quarters.

rifle

The SEALs' wet suits contain an earphone pocket in the hood so divers can communicate underwater.

25

THE SQUADRONS

Delta is believed to have around 1,000 members. Between 250 and 350 of them are trained for action and reconnaissance. They are split into three main operational squadrons. These are further broken down into troops. One troop specializes in reconnaissance, and two troops focus on active fighting. Troops often operate in groups as small as four to six men.

AIR PLATOONS

Supporting the three active squadrons is a helicopter platoon, which includes both attack and transport helicopters. The 160th Special Operations Aviation Regiment (160 SOAR) provides additional air transport. Backup units deal with training, planning, and medical treatment. Delta keeps doctors at their Fort Bragg headquarters in North Carolina, as well as at other secret bases around the United States, to provide medical assistance as needed.

TROOP SUPPORT

Delta's in-house intelligence arm, Operational Support Troop (OST), is also based at Fort Bragg. OST's job is to enter a country secretly ahead of a Delta intervention and send back information on enemy troop numbers and locations. Another important section at Fort Bragg is the Delta training facility. Details are top secret, but it is believed to include shooting ranges, swimming and diving pools, and simulators for all types of locations where terrorists could attack, such as trains and airplanes.

27

BEAR GRYLLS

THE STATS

Name: Edward Michael "Bear" Grylls
Born: June 7, 1974
Place of birth: Donaghadee, Northern Ireland
Job: Adventurer, TV host

TASTE FOR ADVENTURE

Edward Grylls was nicknamed Bear by his older sister when he was just a week old. He has always loved the thrill of adventure. He learned how to sail and climb from his father. As a teenager, he earned a black belt in karate and learned how to skydive.

IN THE SAS

After leaving school, Bear considered joining the Indian army and spent several months hiking in the Himalayas. He eventually joined the British Army instead and passed the SAS selection tests—one of four successful candidates out of 180 entrants. Bear spent three years in the SAS before he broke three vertebrae in a parachuting accident. Doctors told him he came very close to damaging his spinal cord and being paralized for life.

ON TELEVISION

In 2005 Bear's first television series, *Escape to the Legion*, followed him as he trained in North Africa with the French Foreign Legion. Bear's success led to 15 one-hour shows called *Man vs. Wild*. These feature Bear parachuting into some of the world's most dangerous places and showing what you need to do to survive. *Man vs. Wild* became the top cable show in the United States and reached a global audience of more than 1.2 billion. Bear Grylls is a born survivor!

ACTION MAN

Bear spent 18 months rehabilitating. At just 23 years old, he became the youngest British citizen to climb Mount Everest. The 1998 expedition took four months, and Bear was nearly killed when he fell into a 3.6-mile-deep (5,800 m) crack. In 2003 Bear crossed the North Atlantic Ocean in a 36-foot (11 m) inflatable dingy, braving icebergs and massive winds in the world's deadliest stretch of water.

SPECIAL STATS!

80 PERCENT

The average dropout rate during training for special forces recruits.

55,000

The approximate number of special forces personnel in the U.S. military.

45 POUNDS (20 KG)

The weight of the backpack that special forces recruits carry for 40 miles (64 km) as part of their selection procedure. It is equivalent to the weight of an average six-year-old child!

295 FEET (90 M)

The closest to the ground HALO jumpers can be before opening their parachute.

1,000

The number of hours a special forces recruit will spend on the firing range.

1:200

The ratio of U.S. Navy SEAL casualties to enemy casualties during the Vietnam War (1957–1975).

0

Number of U.S. servicewomen serving as SEALs, Rangers, or Green Berets. (Women do have support roles but are not allowed to go on missions.)

30

The number of months it takes to train a U.S. Navy SEAL for the first mission.

GET MORE INFO

Books

Donovan, Sandy. *U.S. Navy Special Warfare Forces*. Minneapolis: Lerner Publications Company, 2005.Check out this book for more info about special ops forces within the navy.

Fridell, Ron. *Military Technology*. Minneapolis: Lerner Publications Company, 2008. This book covers equipment used by the armed forces on land, at sea, and in the air.

Roberts, Jeremy. *U.S. Army Special Operations Forces*. Minneapolis: Lerner Publications Company, 2005. Check out this book for more info about Delta Force and other elite U.S. special ops forces.

Sutherland, Adam. *Armed Services*. Minneapolis: Lerner Publications Company, 2012. This book gives an overview of the work of the various branches that make up the armed forces.

Sutherland, Adam. *Undercover Operations*. Minneapolis: Lerner Publications Company, 2012. Equipment and skills needed for secret ops are covered in this exciting book.

Websites

Navy SEALS
http://www.sealswcc.com/
This is the official site of this elite navy special ops group.

Special Operations
http://www.specialoperations.com/usspecops.html
This site offers lots of info on various U.S. and international special ops groups.

INDEX